JOURNEYS

Reader's Notebook
Volume 1

Grade 2

HOUGHTON MIFFLIN HARCOURT
School Publishers

Contents

Lesson 1
READER'S NOTEBOOK

Short Vowels *a, i*

Henry and Mudge
Phonics: Short Vowels *a, i*

Read each word. Draw a line to the picture that it matches.

1. drag

2. drip

3. fist

4. fast

5. clip

6. clap

Name _____ Date _____

Subjects

> - A **sentence** tells a complete thought. It has a naming part and an action part.
> - The **subject** is the naming part of a sentence.
> - The subject tells who or what does or did something. The subject tells what the sentence is about.
>
> <u>Children</u> play spy games.

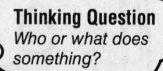

Thinking Question
Who or what does something?

 Draw a line under the naming part of the sentence.

1. Jason sneaks around.

2. Kim looks through windows.

3. My brother writes in a notebook.

4. John reads spy books.

 Write the naming part from the box to finish each sentence.

The cat   Jill

5. _____ tells spy stories.

6. _____ purrs on her lap.

Predicates

> • A **predicate** is the action part of a sentence.
> • A predicate tells what the subject in a sentence does or did.
> • The action part of a sentence uses words that show action.
>
> David (hides toys.)

Thinking Question
What does someone or something in the sentence do?

 Circle the word or words to finish each sentence.

1. Sydney _____.

    looks for clues   **for clues**

2. Tara _____.

    house   **goes into the house**

3. The children _____.

    act like spies   **spies**

4. The kids _____.

    clues   **follow their clues**

5. Everyone _____.

    the toys   **finds the toys**

Name _____   Date _____

Lesson 1
READER'S NOTEBOOK

Focus Trait: Ideas
Adding Details

Henry and Mudge
Writing: Narrative Writing

Without Details	With Details
Jackie's dog liked to play.	Jackie's dog liked to chase sticks and play catch.

Read each sentence without details added. Then rewrite the sentence, using the details in ( ).

1. The day was rainy. (with a cold wind)

_____

2. I took my dog for a walk. (in the park, Duke)

_____

3. I got dressed. (in boots, a raincoat, a big hat)

_____

4. We walked to a place. (near my school, in the park)

_____

5. Duke jumped. (big, into a mud puddle)

_____

CVC Words

Finish writing the name of the picture. One syllable is written for you.

1.

pic _____

2.

_____ bit

3.

_____ zag

4.

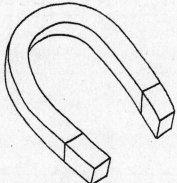

mag _____

5.

ban _____

6.

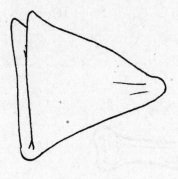

_____ kin

Henry and Mudge

Henry's Journal

Hi, I'm Henry. I started a journal about getting a dog. Help me finish each entry. Use examples from the text and illustrations to help show how I felt.

Read pages 16–17. How did I feel at the beginning of the story?

First, I felt	because

Name _____ Date _____

What Is a Sentence?

Henry and Mudge
Grammar: Subjects and Predicates

 Write the subject to finish each sentence.

1. _____ writes a letter. (Mike, Hold)

2. _____ mails the letter. (Maddie, To)

3. _____ ask for a dog. (Hear, The children)

4. _____ has fun. (Everyone, Throw)

Circle the word or words to finish each sentence.

5. The puppies _____.

   ran in circles   **circles**

6. Henry _____.

   dog   **found a dog**

7. Mudge _____.

   licked Henry   **Henry**

8. Everyone _____.

   patted Mudge   **patted**

Alphabetical Order

Put the words in the box in alphabetical order.

Word Bank

collars	straight	floppy	weighed
big	drooled	dog	curly
row	stood		

1. _____

2. _____

3. _____

4. _____

5. _____

6. _____

7. _____

8. _____

9. _____

10. _____

Sentence Fluency

Short Sentences

Pedro collected toys. Janie collected toys.

New Sentence with Joined Subjects

Pedro and Janie collected toys.

✏️ **Read each pair of sentences. Use *and* to join the two subjects. Write the new sentence.**

1. Miguel wanted to help kids.

Anna wanted to help kids.

_____

2. Mom picked up toys.

Dad picked up toys.

_____

3. Tyler wrapped toys.

Max wrapped toys.

_____

4. Emma took the toys to the shelter.

Jack took the toys to the shelter.

_____

5. The children clapped.

The parents clapped.

_____

Name _____ Date _____

Short Vowels *o, u, e*

Word Bank

tent	skunk	nest	stem
hump	frog	spot	

Write the picture names in the puzzle.

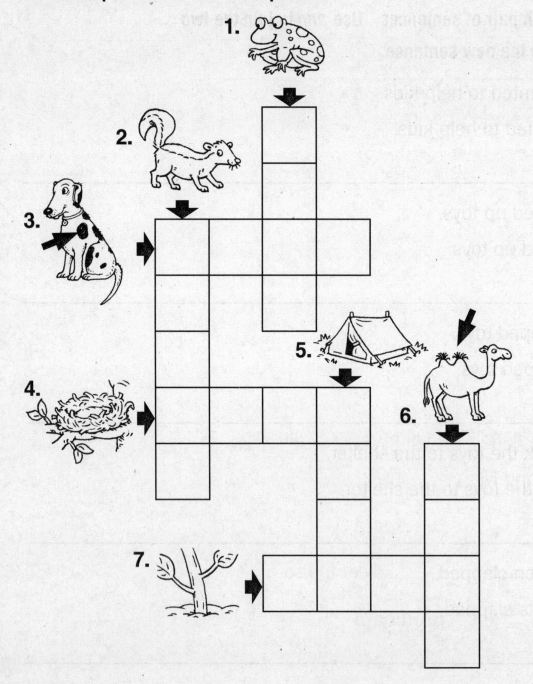

Is It a Sentence?

- A sentence tells what someone or something does or did.
- A **complete simple sentence** has a subject (naming part) and a predicate (action part).

Grandma makes a soup.

Subject: Grandma

Predicate: makes a soup

Thinking Question
What is the subject, or naming part, and what is the predicate, or action part?

 Underline each complete simple sentence.

1. Chops peppers.

Harry chops peppers.

2. Stirs the soup.

Nan stirs the soup.

3. My brother sets the table.

My brother.

 Circle the part of the sentence that is missing.

4. Grandma and Mama _____.

    subject   **predicate**

5. _____ eat the soup.

    subject   **predicate**

Short Vowels *o, u, e*

Word Bank

stop	bump	left
plug	step	up

Write the words on the correct signs.

1.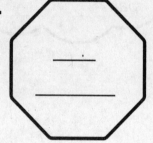

2.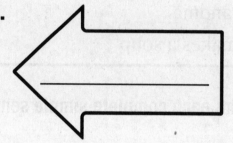

3.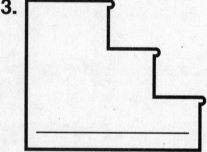

4.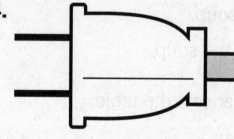

5.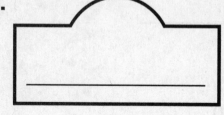

6.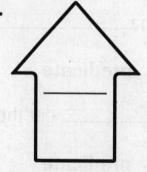

Focus Trait: Voice Expressing Feelings

Without Feelings	With Feelings
My grandma comes to visit on weekends.	**It's always so much fun when** my grandma comes to visit on weekends.

A. Read each sentence. Add words and details to show feelings.

Without Feelings	Feelings Added
1. I liked to help cook dinner.	_____ to help cook dinner.
2. We talk and work hard.	We _____ and work hard.

B. Read each sentence. Then rewrite it to add feelings.

Without Feelings	Feelings Added
3. I live with my family.	
4. I write stories.	
5. I had dinner at my friend Adam's house.	

Review CVC Words

Say the picture name. Draw a line between the syllables.

1.

d e n t i s t

2.

b o b c a t

3.

p e n c i l

4.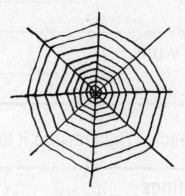

c o b w e b

5.

m a s c o t

6.

l a p t o p

My Family

Thank You Notes to My Family

I am Camila. I want to write notes to thank my family. You can help me write the notes. Use examples from the text and photographs to show how each family member is special to me.

Read page 45. Think about what makes Mom special to me.

Dear Mom,
_____
_____
_____
Love, Camila

Read page 46. Think about what makes Grandma Marta special to me.

Dear Grandma Marta,
_____
_____
_____
Love, Camila

Read page 52. Think about what makes Aunt Martica special to me.

Dear Aunt Martica,

_____

_____

_____

_____

Love, Camila

Read page 57. Think about what makes Papi special to me.

Dear Papi,

_____

_____

_____

_____

Love, Camila

24

Subjects

 Draw a line under the subject in each sentence.

1. Grandma and Grandpa came to visit.

2. The whole family went on a picnic.

3. The park was crowded.

4. The day was warm and sunny.

 Write a subject to complete each sentence.

5. _____ was friendly.

6. _____ took the bus.

Sentence Fluency

Not Complete Sentences

Walks me to school. Uncle Luis.

Complete Sentences

My brother walks me to school.

Uncle Luis picks me up.

Read each word group. Add a subject or a predicate to each group to make a complete sentence. Use the words in the box.

Mom	Aunt Rose
brings us gifts	My sister
makes me laugh	

1. Uncle Luis _____.

2. _____ helps me do homework.

3. _____ sings to me.

4. Papa _____.

5. _____ cooks me dinner.

Long Vowels *a, i*

Word Bank

time	nice	like
slice	cake	bake

Write the word from the Word Bank that completes the sentence.

1.

We can

_____.

2.

It takes

_____.

3.

Look at our

_____!

4.

Here is a

_____.

5.

Do you

_____ it?

6.

It is very

_____!

Statements and Questions

- A **statement** is a sentence that tells something. A statement begins with a capital letter and ends with a period.

- A **question** is a sentence that asks something. A question begins with a capital letter and ends with a question mark.

My dog is very big.

What is your dog's name?

Thinking Questions
Does the sentence tell something or ask something? Does it end with a period or a question mark?

 Write each statement or question correctly.

1. josh and his family have three pets

_____

2. They have a dog and two goldfish

_____

3. where does the dog sleep

_____

4. who takes care of the dog

_____

5. the dog sleeps with Josh

_____

Name _____ Date _____

Commands

- A **command** is a sentence that gives an order.
- A command begins with a capital letter and ends with a period.

Bring your dog to school.

Thinking Question
Does the sentence give an order, begin with a capital letter, and end with a period?

 Write each command correctly.

1. give the dog a treat

_____

2. take your dog to the park

_____

3. teach your dog a trick

_____

4. find a collar for the dog

_____

5. keep your dog quiet

_____

Focus Trait: Word Choice
Sense Words

Without Sense Words	Sense Words Added
I run across the grass.	I run across the <u>wet</u> grass and <u>feel</u> the <u>hot</u> sun.

Read each sentence below. Rewrite each sentence to include sense words.

Without Sense Words	Sense Words Added
1. <u>Outside my window there is a flag.</u>	
2. <u>The bat hits the baseball.</u>	
3. <u>The snow lies on the ground.</u>	
4. <u>The wind blows.</u>	
5. <u>We ate a good dinner.</u>	

Sounds for *c*

Dogs
Phonics: Hard and Soft Sounds
for *c*

Complete the sentences about Cal and Cindy. Use words from the box.

Use words with the /k/ sound for *c* for Cal. Use words with the /s/ sound for *c* for Cindy.

Word Bank

cake	city
mice	rice
camp	cats

Cal

1. Cal has two pet

_____.

2. Cal likes to eat

_____.

3. Cal went to a big

_____.

Cindy

4. Cindy has two pet

_____.

5. Cindy likes to eat

_____.

6. Cindy went to a big

_____.

Name _____ Date _____

Dogs

Create an Adopt-a-Dog Poster

Did you like learning about dogs? Use what you learned to create a poster for an animal shelter. Use examples from the text and illustrations to help you organize facts for your poster.

Read page 79. When can a puppy be adopted?

_____

_____

Read page 85. What do dogs eat?

_____

_____

Read page 86. What do you need to care for a dog?

_____

_____

Read page 88. How do you take care of a dog?

_____

Exclamations

- An **exclamation** is a sentence that shows strong feeling.
- An exclamation begins with a capital letter and ends with an exclamation point.

That dog saved the day!

Thinking Questions
Does the sentence show strong feeling? Does it end with an exclamation point?

 Write each exclamation correctly.

1. People like my dog

_____

2. he is the smartest dog I know

_____

3. My dog chewed my friend's shoe to bits

_____

4. her dog had puppies

_____

5. Those dogs run so fast

_____

Name _____   Date _____

Lesson 3
READER'S NOTEBOOK

Dogs
Vocabulary Strategies:
Multiple-Meaning Words

Multiple-Meaning Words

**Read both definitions of each word. Then read the
sentence. Put a checkmark next to the definition that
best matches the meaning of the underlined word.**

1. pet 1 an animal kept at home ☐

      2 stroke or pat gently ☐

Which do you think makes a better <u>pet</u>, a cat
or a dog?

2. pick 1 take something with your hands ☐

      2 choose something or someone ☐

Joe will <u>pick</u> four people to be on his team.

3. cool 1 cold ☐

      2 neat and interesting ☐

The winter air was <u>cool</u> and windy.

4. kid 1 a child or young person ☐

      2 a young goat ☐

I have liked to read since I was a <u>kid</u>.

5. raise 1 move or lift something higher ☐

      2 make an amount or number bigger ☐

Mr. Jones goes outside to <u>raise</u> the flag at school
each morning.

Proofread for Spelling

Dogs
Spelling: Long Vowels *a, i*

Proofread the story. Circle the six misspelled words.
Then write the correct spellings on the lines below.

   I was working in the yard when Jake and Ken stopped by with a new byke.

   "Is it yours?" I asked Ken.

   "No," Jake said. "It's mien. Do you want to rase?"

   "Yeah, let's!" I answered. I took my rak and made a starting lyne in the dirt. "Ken, you be the judge and give the winner a prise!"

1. _____   4. _____

2. _____   5. _____

3. _____   6. _____

Spelling Words

Basic Words
1. cake
2. mine
3. plate
4. size
5. ate
6. grape
7. prize
8. wipe
9. race
10. line
11. pile
12. rake

Review Words
13. gave
14. bike

Change one letter in each word to make a Spelling Word.

7. ripe _____   10. ape _____

8. slate _____   11. lake _____

9. side _____   12. tile _____

Predicates

 Draw a line under the predicate in each sentence.

1. Her dog ran to greet her.

2. They raised three dogs.

3. We feed our dog eggs.

4. I took my dog for a walk.

 Write a predicate to complete each sentence.

5. The vet _____.

6. The puppies _____.

Kinds of Sentences

> **Statement:** Dave is happy walking his dog.
> **Question:** Is Dave walking his dog?
> **Command:** Walk the dog.
> **Exclamation:** Dave loves walking his dog!

 Change each sentence to another kind of sentence.

The word in ( ) tells what kind of sentence to write.

1. Carlo's dog likes to play catch. (question)

_____

2. Does her dog know how to sit up? (statement)

_____

3. Feed the dog. (question)

_____

4. My dog is a good pet. (exclamation)

_____

5. You need to give the dog a bath. (command)

_____

6. Call your dog. (statement)

_____

Long Vowels *o, u, e*

Read the words in the box. Cross out the words with short vowels. Use the words that are left to complete the jokes.

mole	home	stamp
Luke	blond	rust
hunt	Ken	mask
rose	stone	nose
nest	broke	

What do you get if you toss a big

s_____ into a little lake?

A wet stone!

What smells best at

Jen's h_____?

Jen's n_____!

What did the m_____

say to the r_____?

Hi Bud!

What did L_____ say

when he b_____ his leg

in two spots?

I will never go back

to those two spots!

Name _____ Date _____

Lesson 4
READER'S NOTEBOOK

Nouns for People and Animals

Diary of a Spider
Grammar: What Is a Noun?

A **noun** is a word that names a person or animal. A noun can name one or more than one.
A <u>spider</u> spins a web.

Thinking Question
Which word names a person or animal?

✏️ **Read each sentence. Write the noun that names a person or animal.**

1. The bee plays on the swings.

_____

2. The girls run away.

_____

3. An ant walks on the picnic blanket.

_____

4. The boy eats his lunch.

_____

5. The butterfly has a birthday.

_____

6. The leaf fell on two caterpillars.

_____

Long Vowels *o, u, e*

Add *e* to finish each word.

Then use the words in the puzzle.

Word Bank

pol____   cub____   nos____   rul____

rud____   tun____   ston____   smok____

Across

2. what to do or not do

4. rock

5. a flag is on it

7. can be made of ice

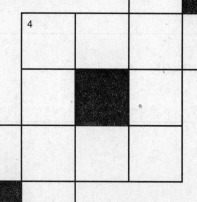

Down

1. sing it

3. smell with it

4. made when paper burns

6. not very nice

Focus Trait: Ideas
Main Idea

All of the sentences in a paragraph should be about the main idea. Below, the writer crossed out a sentence because it was not about the main idea.

Main idea: I went to the park with my sister today.

I went to the park with my sister today. We tried the seesaw. It didn't work. ~~Grampa says that in his day, flies and spiders did not get along.~~ We tried the tire swing. It didn't work, either.

Read the main idea and the details below it. Cross out the detail sentence that does not tell more about the main idea.

1. **Main idea:** I'm sleeping over at my friend's house.

   After dinner, we will watch a movie.
   We will stay up late.
   I forgot my homework today.
   We will tell scary stories.

2. **Main idea:** A big storm is coming this way.

   The wind is blowing things around.
   My friends like to swim in a pool.
   The sky is getting dark.
   Cold rain has already started.

Hard and Soft Sounds for *g*

Complete the sentences. Use words from the box.

```
Word Bank
```

garden	magic	dig	gave
gate	huge	giant	

1. Today Granny _____ me some
   seeds.

2. Now we can start a _____.

3. We start work next to the _____.

4. We will _____ before we plant the seeds.

5. Granny says seeds are like _____.

6. A little seed grows into a _____ plant.

7. I hope our plants grow as big as a _____!

 Reader's Guide

Diary of a Spider

An Interview with Fly

Hello. I'm Fly. I am best friends with Spider. Do you want to know what it is like to have a spider for a friend? Find examples from the text and illustrations to learn about my friendship with Spider.

Read page 109. What do you learn about the friendship on this page?

Spider and Fly _____

_____

Read pages 108 and 118. Look at the illustrations. What do you learn about spiders and flies on this page?

Spiders eat _____ and flies eat with _____

Read pages 118 and 119. What do you learn about the friendship on this page?

Spider _____

Read page 128. What do you learn about the friendship on this page?

Spider and Fly are friends, because _____

_____

A newspaper is interviewing me about my friendship with Spider. Use what you learned to answer their questions.

What do you and Spider like to do?

Spider and I like to _____

_____

What problems do you and Spider have?

Spider and I _____

_____

Why is it nice to have a spider as a friend?

Spider helps me _____

_____

What is the secret to your friendship?

Spider and I take time _____

_____

Statements and Questions

 Write **Statement** or **Question** to identify each sentence.

1. The web is in my tree. _____

2. Did Mom say the web is hers? _____

3. Who said the next bug is mine? _____

4. You can share my tasty treat. _____

 Write each statement or question correctly.

5. who likes the spider's web

_____

6. it looks like my web

_____

Name _____ Date _____

Lesson 4
READER'S NOTEBOOK

Word Choice

Diary of a Spider
Grammar: Connect to Writing

Noun	Exact Noun
animal	spider
place	park

Replace each underlined word with an exact noun from the Word Box below.

The spiders have a picnic. Every bug at the picnic

brings some food. Beetle brings <u>food</u>. Caterpillar brings

                  1

<u>drink</u>. The party is near the <u>flowers</u>. The bugs all sing

 2   3

and dance. They have a great time. <u>Insect</u> must leave

                     4

early. Baby Bee has flying lessons. <u>Bird</u> is the teacher.

                    5

Crow	roses	Bee	pasta	juice

1. _____

2. _____

3. _____

4. _____

5. _____

Grammar
© Houghton Mifflin Harcourt Publishing Company. All rights reserved.
60
Grade 2, Unit 1

Name _____ Date _____

Consonant Blends
with *r, l, s*

Read the words in the box. Underline the blends.

Then use the words to complete Greta's letter.

Word Bank

skate	best	cold	plane
Clare	stripes	smile	froze

Dear _____,

   Soon I will be on a

_____ to your house. I

_____ when I think of it!

How _____ is it there? I

will bring my _____ mittens.

They have _____ on them.

I hope the pond _____!

Then we can _____ on it.

                    Your friend,
                    Greta

One and More Than One

- A **singular** noun names one person, animal, place, or thing.
- A **plural** noun names more than one person, animal, place, or thing.
- Add -*s* to most nouns to make them plural.

She has a <u>pet</u>.   Two <u>pets</u> play.

Thinking Question
*Does the noun
name one or more
than one?*

 Decide if the underlined noun is singular or plural.

1. Many <u>students</u> have pets.

singular   **plural**

2. One <u>cat</u> purrs softly.

singular   **plural**

3. Some <u>crickets</u> are noisy.

singular   **plural**

4. A <u>hamster</u> is furry.

singular   **plural**

5. Three <u>kittens</u> play happily.

singular   **plural**

6. The <u>teacher</u> watches quietly.

singular   **plural**

62

Making Nouns Plural

- Use **plural** nouns when you are talking about more than one.
- Add *-s* to most nouns to name more than one.

Singular	Plural
My <u>cat</u> drank milk.	My <u>cats</u> drank milk.

Thinking Question
Does the noun name one or more than one?

 Change the underlined noun into a plural noun.
Write the new sentence.

1. The <u>pie</u> sat on the table.

_____

2. The <u>smell</u> filled the classroom.

_____

3. The <u>cat</u> jumped.

_____

4. The <u>plate</u> fell to the floor.

_____

5. The <u>girl</u> looked surprised.

_____

6. The <u>pet</u> ran away.

_____

Focus Trait: Sentence Fluency Time-Order Words

Time-Order Words
first, then, last, soon, next, tomorrow, later, last night, today

Read each pair of sentences. Rewrite the sentences by adding the time-order word given.

1. The puppy was tired. It sat down. (Then)

_____

2. It was getting dark outside. It would be time to go home. (Soon)

_____

_____

3. The puppy stood up. It ran home. (Next,)

_____

_____

Write two sentences. Use at least one time-order word.

4. _____

_____

Cumulative Review

Read the clues. Write the correct word on the line.

1. It starts like **plan**.

It rhymes with **lane**.

It goes fast and high.

What is it?

_____

2. It starts like **slid**.

It rhymes with **side**.

You play on it.

What is it?

3. It starts like **cat**.

It rhymes with **page**.

A pet bird can live in it.

What is it?

_____

4. It starts like **stop**.

It has a long **o** sound.

Dad makes dinner
with it.

What is it?

_____

5. It starts like **gas**.

It rhymes with **same**.

It is fun to play.

What is it?

_____

6. It starts like **flag**.

It rhymes with **cute**.

You play a tune on it.

What is it?

_____

Word Bank

gold
stove
slide
game
plane
scrape
flute
cage

Teacher's Pets

Friend to Animals Award

The animal shelter gives an award called "Friend to Animals." Roger thinks Miss Fry should win the award this year. Use examples from the text and illustrations to help show why she should win.

Read page 153 to see how Miss Fry cares for the pets.

Miss Fry cares for the pets by _____

_____

Read page 156 to see how Miss Fry treats the pets.

Miss Fry _____ when Vincent does a trick.

Read page 163 to see how Miss Fry treats the pets.

Miss Fry thinks about _____.

Read page 167 to see how Miss Fry feels about her new pet.

Miss Fry feels _____ when Roger gives her Moe.

Singular and Plural Nouns

 Write the sentences. Use the plural nouns.

1. Two (rabbit, rabbits) run a race.

_____

2. The (turtle, turtles) join in.

_____

3. Many (student, students) laugh.

_____

4. The (pet, pets) run as fast as they can.

_____

 Change the underlined noun into a plural noun.
Write the new sentence.

5. The <u>bird</u> flew in the window.

_____

6. The <u>frog</u> jumped around the room.

_____

7. The <u>snake</u> hissed loudly.

_____

8. The <u>student</u> walked outside.

_____

Name _____   Date _____

Lesson 5
READER'S NOTEBOOK

Teacher's Pets
Vocabulary Strategies:
Word Endings -ed, -ing

Word Endings -ed, -ing

Choose the word that best completes each sentence.
Write the word on the line.

1. Troy and Chad _____ to school yesterday.

walked   **walking**

2. Vicky is _____ Tina on the phone now.

called   **calling**

3. I see two dogs _____ at that cat.

barked   **barking**

4. My grandma _____ with us last summer.

stayed   **staying**

5. Yesterday the teacher _____ us a question.

asked   **asking**

6. Dad took the key and _____ the gate.

locked   **locking**

Conventions

Singular Nouns	Plural Nouns
one lizard	two lizards
a student	many students

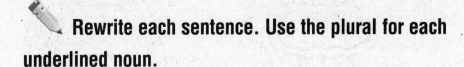 **Rewrite each sentence. Use the plural for each underlined noun.**

1. We saw many <u>pet</u> at school.

   _____

2. Two <u>rabbit</u> lived with the first graders.

   _____

3. Some <u>duck</u> quacked in the second grade class.

   _____

4. Three <u>snake</u> hissed in the third grade class.

   _____

5. The fourth graders fed some <u>spider</u>.

   _____

6. Many <u>animal</u> lived at the school.

   _____

Name _____ Date _____

Common Final Blends
nd, ng, nk, nt, ft, xt, mp

Write the name of each picture. Then circle the final consonant blend.

1. _____

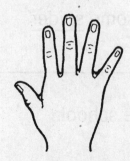

2. _____

3. _____

4. _____

5. _____

6. _____

7. _____

8. _____

9. _____

Adding -*es* to Nouns

- Add -*s* to most nouns to name more than one.

- Add -*es* to nouns that end with *s, x, ch,* and *sh* to name more than one.

one fox   two foxes

Two (fox, <u>foxes</u>) live in a den.

Thinking Question
Do I need a noun that names one, or a noun that names more than one?

Write the correct noun in each sentence. Reread each sentence to make sure that the noun makes sense.

1. The fox den is next to a _____.

   (bush, bushes)

2. Mama Fox wears her _____.

   (glass, glasses)

3. She makes three _____.

   (lunch, lunches)

4. Papa Fox eats one _____.

   (sandwich, sandwiches)

5. Baby Fox eats two _____.

   (peach, peaches)

Name _____ Date _____

Lesson 6
READER'S NOTEBOOK

Animals Building Homes
Phonics: Common Final Blends
nd, ng, nk, nt, ft, xt, mp

Common Final Blends
nd, ng, nk, nt, ft, xt, mp

Answer each pair of clues using the words below them.

1. Coming after: _____

   Went away: _____

   next   **left**

2. A small lake: _____

   To be on your feet: _____

   stand   **pond**

3. To take a sip: _____

   Sleep in a tent: _____

   camp   **drink**

4. Write letters on a page: _____

   Look for something that is lost: _____

   print   **hunt**

5. A tune you can sing: _____

   The sound a horn makes: _____

   honk   **song**

Focus Trait: Ideas
Main Idea and Supporting Details

Main Idea	Supporting Details
Animals need homes.	Keep them safe from enemies Protect them from weather Help them raise babies

Read each set of sentences. Underline the sentence that contains the main idea.

1. Snakes also live in holes.

   Rabbits live underground in warrens.

   Many kinds of animals live in holes.

2. Some people live in apartments.

   People live in different kinds of houses.

   Some people live in ice houses called igloos.

3. They can protect you from harm.

   Dogs make good pets.

   They are loyal.

4. Some mammals live in the water.

   Dolphins look like fish, but they are mammals.

   Sea otters are mammals that live in the Pacific
   Ocean.

Name _____ Date _____

Lesson 6
READER'S NOTEBOOK

Animals Building Homes
Phonics: Cumulative Review

Cumulative Review

Read the words in the box. Write the word that completes each sentence.

Word Bank

| nest | twigs | end |
| spring | play | branches |

1. The _____ of winter is near.

2. It is a sunny day in the _____.

3. Squirrels run and _____.

4. Buds on the _____ will open soon.

5. Two robins build a _____ in the tree.

6. They use _____ and grass to make it strong.

On the lines below, write a word that begins with the beginning blends shown.

7. br _____   9. fr _____   11. st _____

8. pr _____   10. cl _____   12. tr _____

Phonics   82   Grade 2, Unit 2
© Houghton Mifflin Harcourt Publishing Company. All rights reserved.

Name _____ Date _____

Lesson 6
READER'S NOTEBOOK

Animals Building
Homes
Independent Reading

Animals Building Homes

Research Notebook

You are a scientist studying animal homes. Take notes and make sketches in your research log about the different animal homes.

Read page 196. Draw the home you read about. Then write the animal's name and answer the questions.

Animal: _____ How does this animal make its home?

_____

_____

How is the home used?

_____

_____

Read page 202. Draw the home you read about.
Write the animal's name under the drawing.
Then answer the questions.

HOME SWEET HOME

Animal: _____

How does this animal make its home?

_____

_____

How is the home used?

_____

_____

Think with a partner about what you learned. Use your notes to answer the questions.

Why do animals build homes?

_____

_____

Where do animals find materials for building? _____

_____

Parts of a Sentence

✏ **Read each sentence. The action part has one line underneath it. Draw two lines under the naming part.**

1. The cat and dog <u>live</u> in the house.

2. The puppy and kitten <u>play</u> together.

3. A man and woman <u>feed</u> them.

4. A boy and girl <u>pet</u> them.

5. An aunt and uncle <u>visit</u>.

✏ **Read each sentence. The naming part has two lines underneath it. Draw one line under the action part.**

6. <u><u>Tigers and bears</u></u> sleep in caves.

7. <u><u>Turtles and snails</u></u> live in shells.

8. <u><u>Bees and wasps</u></u> make hives.

9. <u><u>Birds and mice</u></u> build nests.

10. <u><u>Gophers</u></u> dig burrows.

Name _____   Date _____

Sentence Fluency

Animals Building Homes
Grammar: Connect to Writing

Short Sentences	New Sentence with Joined Subjects
Foxes live in dens. Bears live in dens.	Foxes and bears live in dens.

Short Sentences	New Sentence with Joined Subjects
Mice make their own nests. Birds make their own nests.	Mice and birds make their own nests.

Read the sentences below. Use *and* to combine their subjects. Write the new sentence on the line.

1. Geese fly to warm places in winter.
   Ducks fly to warm places in winter.

   _____

2. Seals live in cold places.
   Penguins live in cold places.

   _____

3. Squirrels use the branches of trees.
   Crows use the branches of trees.

   _____

4. Baby finches are fed in nests.
   Baby cardinals are fed in nests.

   _____

Double Consonants and *ck*

Read the words below. Think about how the words in each group are alike. Write the missing word that fits in each group.

Word Bank

quack	fluff	dress	duck
mitt	kick	spill	neck

1. pants, shirt, _____

2. fish, frog, _____

3. bat, ball, _____

4. arm, leg, _____

5. tip, splash, _____

6. moo, meow, _____

7. fur, fuzz, _____

8. run, jump, _____

Write a word that rhymes with each word below.

9. stall _____   **11.** back _____

10. mess _____   **12.** will _____

Names for People, Animals, Places, and Things

Some **nouns** name special people, animals, places, or things.. These special nouns are **proper nouns**. Proper nouns begin with capital letters.

Today <u>Lanie Lin</u> plants a garden.

Thinking Question
Which word names a special person, animal, place, or thing?

 Write the proper nouns correctly.

1. She gets help from maggie.

_____

2. We took a field trip to the grand canyon.

_____

3. They plant peas for eric barker.

_____

4. They eat wacky crunch crackers in the garden.

_____

5. They plant carrots for their rabbit hoppy.

_____

Names for Special People and Animals

Some **nouns** name special people or animals. These are **proper nouns**. Names for people and animals begin with capital letters.

Grace fed her cat Fluffy.

Thinking Question
Which word names a special person or animal?

✎ **Rewrite each sentence. Write the name for each special person or animal correctly.**

1. The fitzgeralds grow flowers in their garden.

_____

2. My dog woofy is really loud.

_____

3. Our cat sandy likes to sit in the garden.

_____

4. We brought soup to mrs. crumerine.

_____

5. I like playing catch with mickey.

_____

Focus Trait: Organization
Retelling Events in Order

Events Not in Order	Events in Order
I woke up. I brushed my teeth. I put toothpaste on my toothbrush.	**1.** I woke up. **2.** I put toothpaste on my toothbrush. **3.** I brushed my teeth.

Work with a partner. Number each set of sentences in the order that makes the most sense.

1. ___ I put on my shoes.

___ I put on my socks.

___ I tied my shoes.

2. ___ I had dinner.

___ I had breakfast.

___ I had lunch.

Work on your own. Number each set of sentences in an order that makes sense.

3. ___ The plants started to grow.

___ We planted seeds.

___ We dug up the soil.

5. ___ I went to school.

___ I woke up.

___ I grabbed my lunch.

4. ___ I took out a glass.

___ I poured milk.

___ I drank the milk.

Double Consonants (CVC)

Write a word from the box to complete each sentence below.

Word Bank

happen	bottom	button	cotton	puppet

1. The dress is made of _____.

2. What will _____ if it starts to rain?

3. The children had fun at the _____ show.

4. The rag doll has a _____ for a nose.

5. The prize is at the _____ of the sack.

Answer each clue using a word from the box.

Word Bank

rabbit	kitten	hidden	mitten	muffin

6. Something good to eat _____

7. Another name for a bunny _____

8. It keeps your hand warm. _____

9. A baby cat _____

10. Hard to find _____

Reader's Guide

The Ugly Vegetables

E-mails to Grandma

Hi. I am e-mailing my Grandma to tell her about the garden. Help me finish each e-mail. Use examples from the text and illustrations to show how I feel about the garden.

Read page 233. What can I tell Grandma about the garden?

⊠ re: Garden

How is your garden looking?
Love, Grandma

I am _____ because our plants _____

_____

Read page 237. Now, what can I tell Grandma about the garden?

⊠ re: Garden

How is your garden looking today?
Love, Grandma

I am _____ because our garden _____

_____

Writing Proper Nouns

Rewrite each sentence. Write the name for each special thing correctly.

1. Sue gardens with her deep digger shovel.

_____

2. I gave my dad happy day raisins.

_____

3. I drink giggly grape juice.

_____

Rewrite each sentence. Write the name for each special place correctly.

4. Grapes grow on franklin road.

_____

5. Olives grow in italy.

_____

6. Apples grow in portland.

_____

Homophones

Word Bank

| too | won | wear | plain |
| two | one | where | plane |

Choose the word from the box that best completes the sentence. Write the word on the line.

1. The farmer has _____ shovels.

2. _____ did you put my keys?

3. I don't like stripes or spots. I only like to wear _____ clothes.

4. I am happy because my team _____ the game.

5. My sister is going to the movies. I want to go, _____!

6. I have only _____ flower in the vase.

7. What are you going to _____ to the party?

8. We will take a car to the airport, and then we will get on a _____.

Action Verbs

A **verb** names an action that someone or something does or did.

The wind <u>blows</u> hard.

Thinking Question
Which word names an action?

 Read each sentence. Underline the verb in each sentence.

1. The clouds cover the sky.

2. The rain pours down.

3. People open umbrellas.

4. Water flows down the street.

5. Soon the sun shines.

6. The children play.

7. Children splash in puddles.

8. It rains again after dinner.

9. This time everyone stays dry.

10. Everyone sits inside.

Lesson 8
READER'S NOTEBOOK

Super Storms
Phonics: Consonant Digraphs
th, sh, wh, ch, tch, ph

Words with *th, sh, wh, ch, tch, ph*

Put these letters together to write words with *th, sh, wh, ch, tch,* or *ph.* Then read each word.

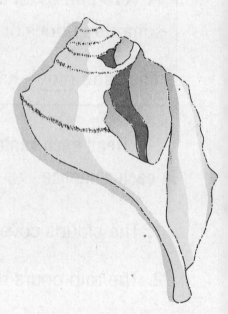

1. c + h + i + p = _____

2. s + h + e + l + l = _____

3. g + r + a + p + h = _____

4. t + h + i + n = _____

5. w + i + s + h = _____

6. w + h + i + t + e = _____

7. m + a + t + c + h = _____

8. p + a + t + h = _____

Write a word you know that begins with each pair of letters.

9. ch _____   11. sh _____

10. th _____   12. ph _____

Name _____ Date _____

Spelling Word Sort

Super Storms
Spelling: Consonant Digraphs *th, sh, wh, ch, tch*

Sort the Spelling Words under the headings below. If a word can sort into more than one place, choose one.

th	sh	wh
_____	_____	_____
_____	_____	_____
_____	_____	_____
_____	_____	

ch

_____

_____

Spelling Words

Basic Words
1. dish
2. than
3. chest
4. such
5. thin
6. push
7. shine
8. chase
9. white
10. while
11. these
12. flash

Review Words
13. which
14. then

Think about the letters *th, sh, wh,* and *ch*. Which Spelling Word could go under two of the headings above?

_____

Name _____ Date _____

Action Verbs and Subjects

A **verb** tells what someone or something does or did. The **subject** tells who or what is doing the action.

The hail <u>pounds</u> on the roof.

Thinking Questions
Which word names an action? Who does or did the action?

Read each sentence. The verb is underlined. Circle the subject.

1. Jan <u>hears</u> the sounds.

2. The cat <u>hides</u> under the bed.

3. The hail <u>bounces</u> on the ground.

4. The clouds <u>turn</u> gray.

Read each sentence. The subject is circled. Underline the verb.

5. The (air) gets cold.

6. (Dan) feels the rain.

7. The (dog) runs through puddles.

8. The (mail) stays dry.

Focus Trait: Word Choice
Definitions

Read each sentence. Draw a line under the definition of the word in dark type.

1. The rain shower became a **thunderstorm**, a storm with heavy rain, thunder, and lightning.

2. They were in the **eye**, or calm center, of the storm.

3. A **blizzard** is a storm with fast winds and heavy snow.

4. The ship was caught in a **hurricane**, a severe tropical storm with winds of more than seventy-five miles per hour.

5. Scientists who follow the path of a storm to study it are called **storm chasers**.

Base Words and Endings
-s, -ed, -ing

Read each word pair. Use the words to answer the clues.

1. prints   **jumps**

Hops up and down _____

Writes words on paper _____

2. lifting   **camping**

Pulling something up _____

Living outside and sleeping in a tent _____

3. packed   **checked**

Looked at something again to be sure _____

Put things in a box or a bag _____

4. passing   **helping**

Doing part of the work _____

Walking by a person or place _____

5. rested   **hunted**

Took a nap _____

Looked for something _____

Super Storms

Write a Storm Poem

Let's look at types of storms. Read the text and study the illustrations. Find details to describe the storms. Then, use those details to write a poem.

Read page 271. Describe a thunderstorm in your own words.

_____

_____

Read page 273. Describe a tornado in your own words.

_____

_____

Read pages 276–278. Describe a hurricane in your own words.

_____

_____

Read page 279. Describe a blizzard in your own words.

_____

_____

Name _____ Date _____

Use your notes to write a poem. Choose a storm that interests you. Answer the questions on the lines. Your answers will make a poem. When you are done, read your poem to a friend.

Which storm did you choose?	_____
What are 2 words to describe the storm?	_____, _____
What are 3 words to describe the storm's actions?	_____, _____, _____
What are 2 words that describe how you would feel in the storm?	_____, _____
What is the name of the storm?	_____

Name _____ Date _____

Base Words and Endings
-ed, -ing

**Read the sentences. Draw a circle around each word
that has the ending -ed or -ing.**

1. Mom is baking a cake for dinner.

2. Dad closed the window when it started to rain.

3. The apple tasted cold and sweet.

4. Jen hoped that her cat was hiding under the bed.

5. The children went hiking last summer.

6. Todd raked the leaves into piles.

**Now write each word you circled under the word that has
the same ending.**

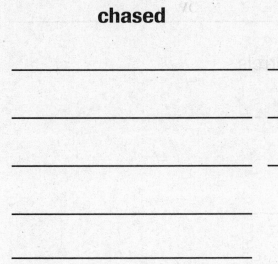

    chased   **riding**

_____ _____

_____ _____

_____ _____

_____

Name _____   Date _____

Lesson 9
READER'S NOTEBOOK

How Chipmunk Got
His Stripes
Grammar: Verbs in the Present

Adding -s to Verbs

A **verb** can name an action that is happening now. Add -s to this kind of verb when it tells about a noun that names one.

The chipmunk eats.

The chipmunks eat.

Thinking Question
Does the subject, or naming part, of the sentence name one or more than one?

 Read each sentence. Then write it correctly.

1. The squirrels (see, sees) the chipmunk.

_____

2. The chipmunk (share, shares) food.

_____

3. A squirrel (run, runs) down the tree.

_____

4. More chipmunks (help, helps) the squirrels.

_____

5. The animals (eat, eats) together.

_____

Name _____   Date _____

Lesson 9
READER'S NOTEBOOK

How Chipmunk Got
His Stripes
Grammar: Verbs in the Present

Adding -*es* to Verbs

A **verb** can tell about an action that is happening now. Add -*es* to this kind of verb if it ends with *s, x, z, ch,* or *sh* and if it tells about a naming part that names one.

The <u>bear</u> mess<u>es</u> the leaf pile.
The <u>bears</u> mess the leaf pile.

Thinking Question
Does the subject name one or more than one?

 Read each sentence. Then write it correctly.

1. The mice (fix, fixes) the pile.

_____

2. The bear (watch, watches) the mice.

_____

3. The bear (push, pushes) the pile down again.

_____

4. The mice (wish, wishes) the bear would stop.

_____

5. The bear (relax, relaxes) on the pile.

_____

Focus Trait: Ideas
Include All Important Steps

Good instructions include all the important steps. Writers leave out
steps that are not important.

**Read the steps for each set of instructions. What step do you
think is missing? Write the missing step.**

Pouring a Glass of Milk

Put a glass on a table.

Go to the refrigerator.

Open the refrigerator door.

_____

Pour the milk carefully.

Making Toast

Get a piece of bread.

Put the bread in the toaster.

Start the toaster.

_____

_____

Spread the butter on the toast.

CV Syllable Pattern

Read each word. Then write the word and draw a slash (/) between the two syllables.

1. pilot _____

2. later _____

3. lemon _____

4. hotel _____

5. tiger _____

Now use the words you wrote above to complete the sentences below.

6. A _____ has orange fur with black stripes.

7. Stan will add _____ to his tea.

8. The _____ sits in the front of the plane.

9. We stayed at a big _____ by the beach last summer.

10. Mom likes to stay up _____ than Dad does.

Name _____ Date _____

Lesson 9
READER'S NOTEBOOK

How Chipmunk Got
His Stripes
Independent Reading

Reader's Guide

How Chipmunk Got His Stripes

Write a Newspaper Article

Newspapers have many different parts. One part is the advice column. In this part, you can write a letter telling your problem. Other people write back telling you what they think you should do. Use examples from the text to help these kids solve their problems.

Read page 311. What would Grandmother tell the writer?

Dear Grandmother,
I told my brother that I run faster than he does. We had a race. I won. I jumped up and down and yelled, "I told you I was faster."
Now he is mad. What should I do?
Dash

_____

Dear Dash,
You should remember _____
_____ I would _____
_____

Love, Grandmother

Name _____ Date _____

Verbs with -*s* and -*es*

Draw a line under the verb that completes each sentence correctly.

1. The bear (walk, walks) through the woods.

2. The snake (slide, slides) on the ground.

3. The rabbit (hop, hops) though the grass.

4. The mouse (run, runs) through the field.

Write the verb correctly to go with the naming part of the sentence.

5. Chipmunk _____ the stew. (mix)

6. Squirrel _____ for a spoon. (reach)

7. Bear _____ to eat. (rush)

8. Bear _____ he had more. (wish)

Synonyms

Read the sentences. Choose the word from the box that means almost the same as the underlined word and write it on the line.

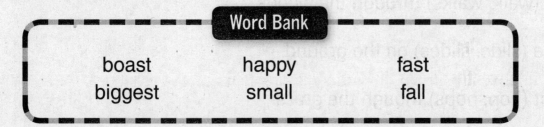

Word Bank

boast	happy	fast
biggest	small	fall

1. In <u>autumn</u>, the leaves change colors.

_____

2. The elephant is the <u>largest</u> animal at the zoo.

_____

3. The mouse is very <u>little</u>.

_____

4. Anita was <u>glad</u> to see her best friend.

_____

5. The runner was <u>quick</u>, so he won the race.

_____

6. Hans likes to <u>brag</u> when he wins a game.

_____

Sentence Fluency

Short Sentences	New Sentence with Joined Predicates
The bear sees honey. The bear eats it all.	The bear sees honey and eats it all.

✏️ **Join each pair of sentences. Use *and* between the predicates. Then write the new sentence.**

1. The squirrels climb the tree.

The squirrels eat some nuts.

_____

2. The deer eats leaves.

The deer drinks from the pond.

_____

3. Chipmunks rest on rocks.

Chipmunks sleep on leaves.

_____

4. The lion runs fast.

The lion looks for food.

_____

Name _____ Date _____

Contractions

Put the words together to write contractions. Then read each contraction.

1. you + are = _____

2. is + not = _____

3. we + will = _____

4. it + is = _____

5. do + not = _____

6. I + am = _____

Use the contractions you wrote above to complete the sentences below.

7. The sun _____ going to shine today.

8. I think _____ going to rain all day.

9. _____ have to stay inside.

10. I hope _____ planning to come over to my house.

11. I _____ know what we can play.

12. _____ sure we can think of something to do.

Name _____ Date _____

Past Tense Verbs with -*ed*

Some **verbs** name actions that are
happening now. Other **verbs** name actions
that happened before now, or in the past. Add
-*ed* to most verbs to show that the
action happened in the past.

Yesterday the jellyfish (float, <u>floated</u>)
in the water.

Thinking Question
*When does or did
the action happen?*

Read each sentence. Choose the verb that tells about
the past. Then rewrite the sentence.

1. Fish (pass, passed) by the jellyfish.

_____

2. Sea turtles (splashed, splash) near the fish.

_____

3. Whales (leap, leaped) over the sea turtles.

_____

4. The sharks (watched, watch) the animals move.

_____

Contractions

Use the two words below the line to make a contraction. Write the contraction on the line. Then read each completed sentence.

1. I _____ know how to skate.
      do not

2. _____ more fun to ride my bike.
      It is

3. I _____ find my knee pads.
      did not

4. _____ try to find my helmet.
      I will

5. Then _____ have fun on our bikes.
         we will

Draw a circle around the contraction in each sentence. Then write the two words for each contraction.

6. I'm going to the store.   _____

7. If you're ready, you can go, too.   _____

8. The store isn't too far away.   _____

9. We'll need to buy milk and meat.   _____

10. I don't think I can carry it on my bike! _____

Focus Trait: Word Choice
Using Exact Words

Jellies
Writing: Informative Writing

Using exact words can make your writing clear
and interesting.

Some jellyfish have a sting that is <u>strong</u>.	Some jellyfish have a sting that is <u>powerful</u>.

**Read each sentence. Replace each underlined word with a
more exact word.**

1. The ocean is a <u>big</u> place.	
2. There are many <u>things</u> in the ocean.	
3. Getting stung by a jellyfish is <u>bad</u>.	
4. Jellyfish are <u>pretty</u>.	
5. Special plants <u>live</u> underwater in the ocean.	

Cumulative Review

Read each sentence. Choose the word from the box
that completes each sentence and write the word on
the line. Then read each completed sentence.

Word Bank

fishing	phone	white	then
wished	chasing	watched	path

1. Dale called jack on the _____.

2. Dale asked if Jack wanted to go _____.

3. The boys walked along a _____.

4. Jack _____ they would get to
   the lake soon.

5. Just _____, a rabbit ran by.

6. The bunny flashed its _____ tail.

7. Dale _____ it run by.

8. Was someone _____ it?

**Now write on the line a word you know that begins with each
letter pair.**

9. ch _____   10. sh _____

Reader's Guide

Jellies: The Life of Jellyfish

Draw and Label a Jellyfish Picture

Let's review some facts about jellyfish. Then, you can use these facts to help you draw a picture of a jellyfish.

Read pages 338–339. What do jellyfish do?

_____

_____

Read page 346. What are some parts of a jellyfish? What are jellyfish shaped like?

_____

_____

Read page 347. What does the author think jellyfish look like when they wash up on the beach?

_____

Read page 348. What does the author think jellyfish look like in the sea?

_____

Did you see a jellyfish that you thought was really interesting? Draw a picture of the jellyfish below. Make labels near parts of the jellyfish and tell how the jellyfish looks and acts.

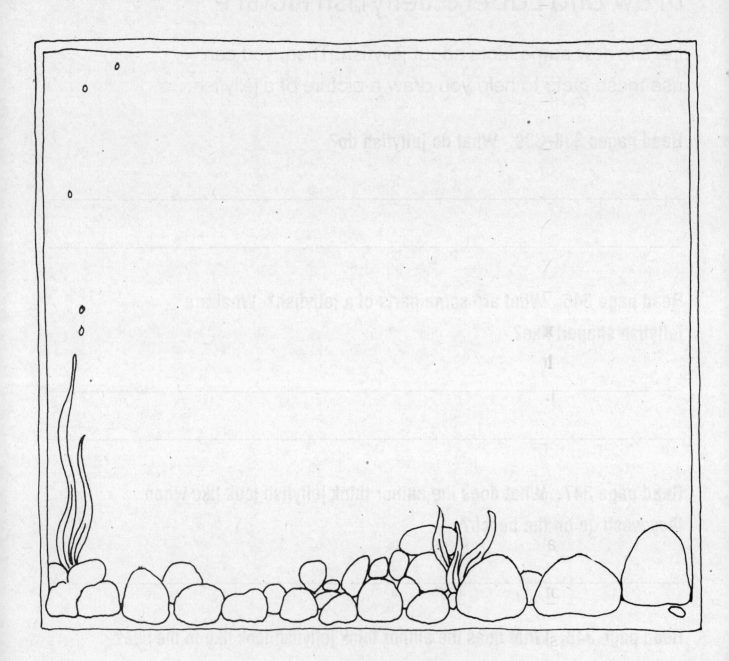

Suffixes -er, -est

Circle the comparing word that completes each sentence.

1. A mouse is **smaller   smallest** than a cat.

2. I am going to exercise so I can get **stronger   strongest**.

3. That is the **bigger   biggest** spider I have ever seen!

4. Being sick made me feel **weaker   weakest** than I did before.

5. Juan wants to be the **smarter   smartest** student in the class.

6. That side of the pool is **shallower   shallowest** than this side.

7. Chocolate is the **sweeter   sweetest** kind of ice cream.

Proofread for Spelling

Rewrite each sentence. Use two contractions in each sentence.

1. I am sure he did not see me.

_____

2. That is where you are going.

_____

3. It is our class picnic, so we will go early.

_____

Spelling Words
Basic Words
1. I'm
2. don't
3. isn't
4. can't
5. we'll
6. it's
7. I've
8. didn't
9. you're
10. that's
11. wasn't
12. you've

Proofread the note. Cross out the six misspelled contractions. Spell each word correctly in the margin.

Dear Pam,

     I kan't go tomorrow because I'ave got too much homework. I know yo'uve been counting on me. Maybe I can come over later in the evening. Then wi'll have time to talk. I hope its' OK. I'am going to start my math problems right now.

                Sincerely,

                Carmen

Singular and Plural Nouns

Draw a line under the noun in each sentence.
If the noun names one, write *S* for *singular*. If the noun
names more than one, write *P* for *plural*.

1. The sharks swim fast. _____

2. Four girls watch. _____

3. One boy points. _____

4. A girl looks again. _____

5. The animals are gone now. _____

Read each sentence. Then rewrite each underlined
noun in the correct plural form.

6. Look at the crab. _____

7. Do not touch the claw. _____

8. Tell the adult to come quickly. _____

9. The boy can use help. _____

10. The crabs crawled in the bag. _____

Sentence Fluency

Verbs Telling About Different Times	Verbs Telling the Same Time
Last week Jill and Jake <u>walked</u> on the beach. They <u>play</u> in the water.	Last week Jill and Jake <u>walked</u> on the beach. They <u>played</u> in the water.

Read this story. It tells about something that happened in the past. Five verbs do not tell about the past. Fix these five verbs. Then write the story correctly on the lines below.

    Jill and Jake skipped along the shore. Jake saw two large shells. Jake point to them. Jill rush over to see them. Jill and Jake look closely. Jill pick up one shell. Jill and Jake wash the shells and took them home.

_____

_____

_____

_____

_____

_____

Name _____ Date _____

Unit 2
READER'S NOTEBOOK

Poppleton in Winter
Segment 1
Independent Reading

Reader's Guide

Poppleton in Winter

Interview with Patrick

Read pages 11–15. If news reporters interviewed Patrick about his day, what would he say? Read the questions below. Write the answers Patrick would give. Include details from the text and illustrations.

Interview with Patrick

1. What problem did you have at Poppleton's house today?

_____

_____

_____

2. When did you have this problem?

_____

_____

_____

Name _____ Date _____

Unit 2
READER'S NOTEBOOK

Poppleton in Winter
Segment 1
Independent Reading

Now answer questions about the events from Poppleton's point of view. Include details from the text and illustrations on pages 11–15.

Interview with Poppleton

1. Why was it a good thing that the icicles were still frozen?

_____

_____

_____

2. Patrick told us that you built a fence. How did you do that?

_____

_____

_____

_____

Name _____ Date _____

Unit 2
READER'S NOTEBOOK

Poppleton in Winter
Segment 2
Independent Reading

Reader's Guide

Poppleton in Winter

Letters to a Friend

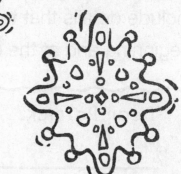

In Chapter 1, Poppleton met Patrick. Now Poppleton wants to write letters to his friend Patrick.

Read pages 18–35. Imagine you are Poppleton. Write a letter to Patrick. Tell him how you made the bust of Cherry Sue. Use details from the text and illustrations.

Dear Patrick,

_____

_____

_____

_____

_____

_____

Your friend,
Poppleton

Name _____ Date _____

Read pages 36–48. Write another letter from Poppleton. Tell Patrick about your birthday. Include details that tell how you felt at the beginning and at the end of the day.

Dear Patrick,

_____

_____

_____

_____

_____

_____

_____

Your friend,
Poppleton

Base Words and Endings -s, -es

Put the letters together to write a base word.
Then add the ending -s or -es.

1. m + a + t + c + h = _____

2. b + u + z + z = _____

3. g + l + a + s + s = _____

4. b + u + s + h = _____

5. h + a + m + m + e + r = _____

**Now use the words you wrote above to complete the
sentences below.**

6. Dad _____ the nails into
   the wall.

7. I drank two _____ of milk
   for dinner.

8. Today my jacket _____ my hat.

9. My dog likes to hide in the _____ .

10. The bee _____ near the hive.

Compound Sentences

- A **compound sentence** is made up of two shorter sentences joined by <u>and</u>, <u>but</u>, or <u>or</u>.

The cows got blankets, but Duck kept the typewriter.

- A comma is used before the joining word.

Thinking Question
Is the sentence made up of two shorter sentences joined by and, but, *or* or?

Draw a line under each shorter sentence in the compound sentences.

1. The cows wanted blankets, and Farmer Brown said, "No way."

2. The cows went on strike, and Farmer Brown was upset.

3. The hens had nests, but they were still cold.

4. Farmer Brown needs milk and eggs, or he can't run his farm.

5. Duck took the typewriter, and he decided to keep it.

Compound Sentences

- A **compound sentence** is made up of two shorter sentences joined by <u>and</u>, <u>but</u>, or <u>or</u>.

- A comma is used before the joining word.

The cows found an old typewriter.

The cows learned to type.

The cows found an old typewriter, and they learned to type.

Thinking Question
How can sentences be combined to make writing less choppy?

Write each pair of sentences as a compound sentence. Use a comma and a joining word.

1. The ducks need a diving board. The ducks will be bored.

_____

_____

2. The ducks liked to swim. The ducks preferred to dive.

_____

_____

3. Duck knocked on the door. Duck handed Farmer Brown a note.

_____

_____

Focus Trait: Ideas
Stating a Clear Goal

Not a Clear Goal	Clear Goal
I would like you to <u>do something.</u>	I would like you to **take me to the park next weekend.**

A. Read each goal that is not clear. Fill in the blanks to state
each goal more clearly.

Not a Clear Goal	Clear Goal
1. I would like you to buy <u>something</u> for our computer lab.	I would like you to buy _____ for our computer lab.
2. I want you to send me <u>stuff</u> for a project.	I want you to send me _____ for a project.

B. Read each goal that is not clear. Add a word or words to
make the goal more clear. Write your new sentences.

Not a Clear Goal	Clear Goal
3. We would like you to <u>do us a favor.</u>	
4. I am writing to ask you <u>to do something</u> for the music room.	

Name _____ Date _____

Lesson 11
READER'S NOTEBOOK

**Click, Clack, Moo:
Cows That Type**
Phonics: Cumulative Review

Cumulative Review

Write the word that goes in each sentence.

Word Bank

cider   fever   later   virus

1. Jack has a _____ that makes
   him sick.

2. Mom says his _____ is very
   high.

3. "You can sit with Jack _____
   today," said Mom.

4. "I'll warm up some _____ for
   both of you," said Mom.

Write the words that make up each underlined contraction.

5. "I won't have lunch with Sam today," said Jack.

   _____

6. "I'll tell Sam you miss him, Jack," I said.

   _____

7. "You're a good sister," said Jack.

   _____

 **Reader's Guide**

Click, Clack, Moo:
Cows That Type

Make a Cartoon

The animals used the typewriter to tell Farmer
Brown what they wanted. Read the text to find
out what each animal said.

Read pages 379–381. What did the cows tell Farmer Brown?

_____

_____

**Read pages 383–384. What did the hens want Farmer Brown
to know?**

_____

_____

Read page 391. What did the ducks tell Farmer Brown?

_____

_____

Which was your favorite animal? What if Farmer Brown and that animal could talk to each other? What would they say? Use the examples from the text and illustrations you found to make a cartoon. Use speech bubbles to show what Farmer Brown and the animal might say.

Base Words with Endings -*s*, -*es*

Write the Spelling Word or Spelling Words that match each clue.

1. These are animals. _____

_____ _____

2. You can eat these. _____

_____

3. Put things inside these. _____

4. Put food on these. _____

5. Ride on these. _____

6. These ring. _____

7. These are airplanes. _____

8. You hope these come true. _____

9. Girls sometimes wear these. _____

10. Put these on letters. _____

11. We give pets these. _____

Spelling Words

**Basic
Words**
1. hens
2. eggs
3. ducks
4. bikes
5. boxes
6. wishes
7. dresses
8. names
9. bells
10. stamps
11. dishes
12. grapes

**Review
Words**
13. jets
14. frogs

Compound Sentences

- A **compound sentence** is made up of two shorter sentences.
- The two shorter sentences are joined by <u>and</u>, <u>but</u>, or <u>or</u>.
- A comma is used before the joining word.

Farmer Brown was angry. Farmer Brown finally made a deal with the cows.

Farmer Brown was angry, but he finally made a deal with the cows.

 Write each pair of sentences as a compound sentence.

1. The animals tried to listen. The animals couldn't understand Moo.

_____

_____

2. The cows had a meeting. The cows decided what to do.

_____

_____

3. The cows needed to be happy. The cows wouldn't give milk.

_____

_____

Prefixes *pre-* and *mis-*

Read each definition below. Add *mis-* or *pre-* to a word in the box to make a new word that matches each definition.

Word Bank

heard	judge	read
order	heat	

1. to order before _____

2. to judge badly _____

3. to heat before _____

4. did not read right _____

5. did not hear right _____

Write a sentence for each word.

6. misdial _____

_____

_____

7. precut _____

_____

Proofread for Spelling

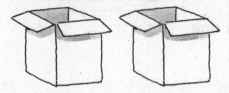

Click, Clack, Moo:
Cows That Type

Spelling: Base Words with
Endings -*s*, -*es*

**Proofread the newspaper story. Circle the nine
misspelled words. Then write the correct spellings.**

Wishs Come True

Mr. and Mrs. Smith kept birds in a pen. Saturday, they
rode their biks. Then they checked the pen. They found
only empty boxees. "I wanted to ring alarm belz," said Mr.
Smith. "I wish that we would find our birds."

When they went inside the house, they found the
duks sleeping on Mrs. Smith's dreses, and the henz had
laid egs on her new dishis!

1. _____   6. _____

2. _____   7. _____

3. _____   8. _____

4. _____   9. _____

5. _____

Unscramble the letters to spell a Basic Word.

10. pgares _____   **12.** pmasts _____

11. maens _____

Spelling Words
Basic Words
1. hens
2. eggs
3. ducks
4. bikes
5. boxes
6. wishes
7. dresses
8. names
9. bells
10. stamps
11. dishes
12. grapes

More Plural Nouns

 Circle the noun that correctly shows more than one.

1. We eat (sandwichs, sandwiches) in the barn.

2. Our (dresss, dresses) get dirty.

3. The (mouses, mice) play in the hay.

4. The (horse, horses) stomp their feet.

5. The (cow, cows) stand still.

Read each sentence. Then rewrite each sentence to use the correct plural form of the underlined noun.

6. Two <u>fox</u> visit the farm.

_____

7. Many <u>man</u> help plant seeds.

_____

8. How many <u>child</u> are in your school?

_____

Compound Sentences

Short, Choppy Sentences	Compound Sentence
Cows give us milk. Hens lay eggs.	Cows give us milk, and hens lay eggs.

  Write each pair of sentences as a compound sentence.

Use a comma and a joining word.

1. The cows can type. The cows can't dance.

_____

_____

2. The cows want electric blankets. The ducks want a diving board.

_____

_____

3. The cows will get blankets. The cows will stay cold.

_____

_____

4. The ducks can dive. The ducks need a board.

_____

_____

Words with *ai, ay*

Write a word from the box to complete each sentence.

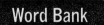

Word Bank

| pail | maybe | say |
| tail | play | wait |

1. I like to _____ games with my dog Spot.

2. "Come here, Spot," I _____.

3. Spot jumps up and wags his _____.

4. _____ Spot will run after a ball.

5. I toss the ball, and it lands in a _____.

6. Spot fetches the ball while I _____ for him.

Now write each word under the word that has the same pattern for long *a*.

mail   **day**

_____   _____

_____   _____

_____   _____

Compound Sentences

- A **compound sentence** is two simpler sentences joined by a comma and the word <u>and</u>, <u>but</u>, or <u>or</u>.

- Moving words around and adding details in a compound sentence can make the sentence more interesting.

Thinking Question
How does moving words around and adding details make sentences more interesting?

Less interesting

I like to sing, and I like to dance.

More interesting

I like to sing popular songs, and I think dancing is fun.

✏ **Move words around and add details to make these compound sentences more interesting.**

1. Shawn plays the guitar, or Shawn plays the drum.

_____

_____

2. Kim plays the piano, but Kim wants to play the organ.

_____

_____

3. We like classical music, and we like jazz.

_____

_____

Words with *ai, ay*

Read the letter. Draw a circle around the words with *ai* and *ay*. Then write two sentences to finish the letter. Choose two words from the box to use in your sentences.

Word Bank

rain	hail	day	may
gray	mail	pay	trail

Dear Jay,

Today my class went on a trip. I could not wait! We saw people make crafts. A man made pots out of clay. One woman wove a braid for a rug. The people sell their crafts and then they get paid. _____

_____

_____

_____

Your friend,

_____

Focus Trait: Voice
Showing Feelings

Weak Voice	Strong Voice
I like movie music.	Movie music is so great to listen to!

A. Read each sentence that has a weak voice. Add or change some words to make the voice stronger.

Weak Voice	Strong Voice
1. The guitar is a musical instrument.	The guitar is a _____ musical instrument.
2. I like all music.	Any kind of music _____ _____

B. Read each sentence that has a weak voice. Add words to make the voice stronger. Include a reason for the opinion. Write your new sentences.

Weak Voice	Strong Voice
3. Our band played a concert.	_____ _____
4. The trumpet is a good instrument.	_____ _____

Cumulative Review

Write the word that goes in each sentence.

Word Bank

| snails | boxes | glasses | bikes |

1. "I can't lift these big _____ of books," said Meg.

2. "We'll ride our _____ to school," Rick said.

3. "I've filled three _____ with milk," said Max.

4. "You're moving at the speed of _____ this morning," Mom said.

Now write each word from the Word Bank under the word that has the same ending.

paints   patches

_____   _____

_____   _____

Ah, Music!

Think Like a Musician

A heading tells you about the text that follows it.
For example, the heading on page 412 is "Music
Is Sound." That section tells about sounds in
music. Write each heading and tell what you learn.

Read page 413. What is the heading on this page?

_____

What did this section teach you about rhythm?

_____

Read page 414. What is the heading on this page?

_____

What did this section teach you about melody?

_____

Read page 416. What is the heading on this page?

_____

What did this section teach you about feeling in music?

_____

Now teach others. Based on details from the text, think like a musician. Pretend a friend is going to a performance. Give your friend advice about rhythm, melody, and feeling in music. Remember you can find information in the book by using headings.

When you go to a music performance, listen for these things.

1. Rhythm: _____

_____

_____

2. Melody: _____

_____

_____

3. Feeling in music: _____

_____

_____

Writing Proper Nouns

🖊 **Write the proper noun in each sentence correctly on the line.**

1. My friend jessica plays the flute. _____

2. The concert is in chicago. _____

3. She will bring her dog willy. _____

4. After the concert we'll have juicy jelly smoothies.

_____

🖊 **Read each sentence. Choose the correct proper noun to replace the underlined words. Write the new sentence on the line.**

5. The woman loves the piano. (Carmen, Canada)

_____

6. She plays it for her fish. (New Mexico, Bubbles)

_____

7. She feeds her fish its food. (Fin Flakes, Main Street)

_____

8. Carmen and Bubbles live on drake road. (Florida, Drake Road)

_____

Compound Sentences

Moving words around and adding details in a compound sentence can make the sentence more interesting.

Less Interesting	More Interesting
Do you like vocals, or do you like instrumentals?	So you like vocals, or are instrumentals your favorite?
My brother only listens to pop, and my sister only listens to country.	My brother only listens to popular music, and country music is all my sister wants to hear.

 Move words around and add details to each sentence.

1. Mom plays the guitar, and Mom is teaching Manny.

_____

_____

2. Shawn is a singer, but Shawn is not a dancer.

_____

_____

3. Do you enjoy concerts, or do you find concerts too loud?

_____

_____

Words with *ee, ea*

Write a word for each clue.

1. It rhymes with *see.*

It begins like *bat.* _____

2. It rhymes with *beaches.*

It begins like *pig.* _____

3. It rhymes with *sweet.*

It begins like *mail.* _____

4. It rhymes with *sheep.*

It begins like *kitten.* _____

5. It rhymes with *beast.*

It begins like *fox.* _____

6. It rhymes with *clean.*

It begins like *bay.* _____

Use two of the words you wrote above in sentences of your own.

7. _____

8. _____

Using Quotation Marks

When you write, show what someone says by putting **quotation marks (" ")** at the beginning and end of the speaker's exact words.

Luis said, "I play the drums."
Kim said, "I play the guitar."

Thinking Question
What are the speaker's exact words?

✏ **Write each sentence. Put quotation marks around the speaker's exact words.**

1. Jamal asked, Will you play for me?

_____

2. Luis said, We will play for you.

_____

3. Kim asked, Do you play, too?

_____

4. Jamal answered, I play the piano.

_____

5. The kids said, Come play with us!

_____

Quotation Marks

Follow these rules when you use quotation marks.

1. Put a **comma** after words such as *said* and *asked*.

2. Begin the first word inside the quotation marks with a **capital letter**.

3. Put the **end mark** inside the quotation marks.

Example: Jenna said, "I wrote a poem."

Thinking Question
Where do the speaker's exact words begin and end?

 Draw a line under the sentence that is written correctly.

1. Maddy asked, "Are you an artist?"

Maddy asked, "are you an artist?"

2. Jenna said "I am a writer."

Jenna said, "I am a writer."

3. Maddy asked, "Are poems hard to write?"

Maddy asked, "Are poems hard to write"

4. Jenna said, "poems are fun to write."

Jenna said, "Poems are fun to write."

Focus Trait: Word Choice
Using Exact Words

Overused Words	Exact Words
Painting is a <u>fun</u> <u>thing</u>.	Painting is an **artistic hobby**.

**A. Read each sentence on the left side. Add or change words
to make them more exact.**

Overused Words	Exact Words
1. Lunch is <u>the best part</u> of the day.	Lunch is _____ of the day.
2. At lunch, I can <u>talk</u> with <u>people</u>.	At lunch, I can _____ with _____.

**B. Read each sentence with overused words. Add or change
words to make them more exact. Write your new sentences.**

Few Exact Words	Add Exact Words or Phrases
3. My art teacher is <u>good</u>.	
4. I love <u>making</u> <u>stuff</u>.	

Cumulative Review

Read each word. Add *-s* or *-es* to each base word.
Then write the new word.

1. rain _____

2. peach _____

3. train _____

4. pail _____

5. fox _____

6. wash _____

7. teach _____

8. catch _____

9. glass _____

10. stain _____

11. box _____

12. buzz _____

Name _____ Date _____

Lesson 13
READER'S NOTEBOOK

Schools Around
the World
Independent Reading

Schools Around the World

Create Your Own School

There were many different schools in the story.
Some were like your school, and some were different.

Read page 441. How are all schools the same?

_____

Read page 442. How are school buildings different?

_____

Read page 443. What are some ways students get to school?

_____

Read page 444. How do children dress at school?

_____

Read pages 445–447. What are some things children do at school?

_____

Quotation Marks

 Write each sentence correctly.

1. Mrs. Smith said, Artists mix colors.

_____

2. Greg said, I will mix blue and yellow.

_____

3. Annie said, You will make green!

_____

 Draw a line under the sentence that is written correctly.

4. Jamie said "I made a basket."

Jamie said, "I made a basket."

5. Robin asked, "how did you do it"?

Robin asked, "How did you do it?"

6. Jamie answered, "I made it out of straw."

Jamie answered ",I made it out of straw."

Using a Dictionary

Read the names for parts of a dictionary entry. Then read the dictionary entry. Write in the boxes the labels for the parts of the dictionary entry.

example sentence   part of speech   pronunciation

word meaning   entry word

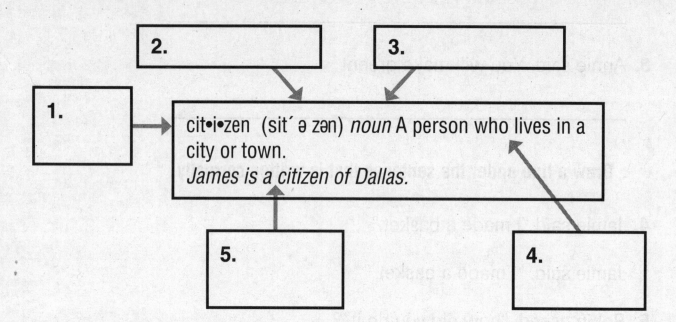

2.

3.

1.

cit•i•zen (sit´ ə zən) *noun* A person who lives in a city or town.
James is a citizen of Dallas.

5.

4.

6. Write two good reasons to use a dictionary.

_____

_____

Name _____ Date _____

Lesson 13
READER'S NOTEBOOK

Schools Around
the World
Grammar: Connect to Writing

Conventions

Sentences Written Incorrectly	Sentences Written Correctly
Jimmy asked "Is that a clay bowl?" Mom said. "yes, I made it in art class."	Jimmy asked, "Is that a clay bowl?" Mom said, "Yes, I made it in art class."

Write each sentence correctly. Fix mistakes in capitalization and punctuation. Put the quotation marks where they belong.

1. Mom asked "Do you want to come to art class?

_____

2. I asked, what will we do?"

_____

3. "mom answered this week we will make puppets"

_____

4. I said "That sounds like fun!

_____

5. She said Next week we will put on a puppet show!"

_____

Long *o* (*o, oa, ow*)

Write a word for each clue.

Word Bank

zero   clover   coast
groan   gold   glow

1. It rhymes with **toast.**

It begins like **cap.** _____

2. It rhymes with **loan.**

It begins like **grapes.** _____

3. It rhymes with **fold.**

It begins like **gap.** _____

4. It rhymes with **show.**

It begins like **glad.** _____

5. It rhymes with **hero.**

It begins like **zip.** _____

6. It rhymes with **over.**

It begins like **clip.** _____

Name _____ Date _____

Name _____ Date _____

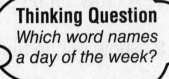

Days of the Week

- There are seven days in a week.
- The names of the days of the week begin with **capital letters**.

Monday	**Thursday**	**Saturday**
Tuesday	**Friday**	**Sunday**
Wednesday		

Bonnie teaches sign language on <u>Tuesday</u>.

Thinking Question
Which word names a day of the week?

 Write each sentence correctly.

1. Bonnie teaches Jessica on wednesday.

_____

2. Jessica has a piano lesson on Tuesday.

_____

3. Jessica mails Bonnie a card on Friday.

_____

4. On monday Bonnie gets the card in the mail.

_____

5. On saturday Bonnie sends Jessica a card.

_____

Long *o (o, oa, ow)*

**Read the sentences. Draw a circle around each word
that has the long *o* sound spelled *o, oa,* or *ow*.**

1. A crow sat on the branch of the old oak tree.

2. Snow began to fall on a cold winter day.

3. Throw a stick in the water and see if it floats.

4. You can fold your own paper and put it away.

5. I know that the coach has a gold ring.

**Now write each word you circled under the word that
has the same spelling for long *o*.**

told	**loan**	**blow**
_____	_____	_____
_____	_____	_____
_____	_____	_____
_____		_____

Focus Trait: Ideas
Facts and Opinions

A **fact** can be proved. An **opinion** cannot be proved. An opinion tells what someone thinks or feels. Words such as I think, I like, or I believe are used to show opinions.

✏️ **Read the paragraphs below. Write the opinion from each one. Write two facts that support each opinion.**

Helen Keller learned to read, write, and speak. I believe she was a remarkable person. She traveled around the world. She spoke to large crowds of people.

Opinion: _____

_____

Facts: _____

_____

Annie Sullivan was Helen Keller's teacher. In the beginning, Helen fought with Annie. She even knocked out one of Annie's teeth. I think Helen was a real challenge for Annie.

Opinion: _____

Facts: _____

_____

Cumulative Review

Answer each pair of clues using the words below the clues.

1. A place with sand by a lake or sea _____

   A big meal _____

   beach   **feast**

2. Make a trip in a boat _____
   The feeling you have when you cut your hand

   _____

   pain   **sail**

3. Show someone how to do something _____
   Stretch out your arm to grab something

   _____

   teach   **reach**

4. How fast a car or truck is going _____

   A long way down under water _____

   deep   **speed**

5. To stay in one place until something happens

   _____

   A path that you hike along _____

   trail   **wait**

Helen Keller

Make a Speech

When Helen Keller grew up, she gave speeches. Now you will write a speech about Helen Keller's life.

Read page 475. What was it like for Helen Keller to grow up blind and deaf?

_____

Read pages 476–477. What problems did Helen Keller have?

_____

_____

Read pages 482–485. How did Helen learn to communicate?

_____

_____

Read pages 486–487. What other ways did Helen learn?

_____

_____

After you gave the speech to your friends, they asked you questions. Use details from the text and illustrations to help you answer their questions.

Read page 475. How did Helen become blind and deaf?

1. _____

Read pages 476–478. Could Helen communicate at all before she learned to finger spell?

2. _____

_____

Read pages 481–484. How did Helen learn to spell?

3. _____

_____

_____

Read page 489. How did Helen become so famous?

4. _____

_____

_____

Present and Future Time

- Add *-s* to the end of the verb when it tells about a noun that names one. Add *-es* to verbs ending with *s, x, ch,* and *sh* when they tell about a noun that names one.

Examples: The boy <u>jumps</u>. The egg <u>hatches</u>.

- Add *will* before the verb to tell about an action that will happen in the future.

Draw a line under the correct verb.

1. The coach (teach, teaches) the girl.

2. The child (read, reads) in Braille.

3. The man (fix, fixes) their answers.

Write each sentence correctly to show future time.

4. Carlos reach for a pen.

_____

5. Mary wash her hands before dinner.

_____

6. Ben pass the ball to me.

_____

Using Proper Nouns

Without Words That Tell When	With Words That Tell When
Ben visits me. He hurt his leg. I made a card for him.	Ben visits me <u>every Saturday</u>. He hurt his leg <u>on June 12, 2012</u>. I made a card for him <u>on Valentine's Day</u>.

Read the paragraph. Add phrases from the box to tell when. Write the phrases on the lines.

next Presidents' Day	last Thanksgiving
September 16	every Thursday

Sarah teaches sign language. She started to teach

on _____, 2012. She teaches two

classes at my school _____. She did sign

language for a school play _____.

She will do it again for the play coming up

_____.

Lesson 15
READER'S NOTEBOOK

Compound Words

Officer Buckle and Gloria
Phonics: Compound Words

Read the letter. Draw a circle around each compound word.

Dear Grandfather,

    This afternoon I went to the playground with some

kids from my classroom. We played baseball until

sunset. It was so much fun! Then I went inside to do

my homework. I went upstairs and saw the photo of us

at the seashore in the summertime. I still have the

seashell we found there!

Love,

Julia

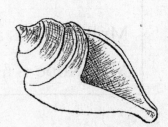

Write a compound word you know on each line.

_____   _____   _____

Titles for People

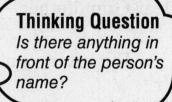

- A **title** may be used before a person's name.
- A title begins with a capital letter and usually ends with a period.

Mr. Ramon is a music teacher.

Miss Kobe is a crossing guard.

Thinking Question
Is there anything in front of the person's name?

 Write each underlined title and name correctly.

1. Our teacher miss Mullen asks a police officer to visit.

_____

2. On Mondays mr Ramon comes to our class.

_____

3. He brings his partner, mrs Shay.

_____

4. They come with dr Lucky.

_____

5. They talk with the coach, ms Smith.

_____

216

Name _____ Date _____

Lesson 15
READER'S NOTEBOOK

Officer Buckle
and Gloria
Writing: Opinion Writing

Focus Trait: Organization
Topic Sentences

A good persuasive essay has a goal, reasons, facts, and examples. The **goal** is what the writer wants. **Reasons** tell why. **Facts** and **examples** give more information about the reason.

Read the persuasive essay. Write the goal. Circle the reasons. Underline facts and examples.

Why We Need Officer Buckle and Gloria

I have a great idea! Officer Buckle and Gloria should speak at our school.

One reason is that we all need to learn about safety. Safety tips can keep us from hurting ourselves. They can even save lives!

Another reason is that Officer Buckle and Gloria put on a great show! Gloria acts out all the safety tips. Kids love watching Gloria!

So please, let's invite Officer Buckle and Gloria to speak at our school. I think it would be great!

Goal: _____

What reason does the second paragraph tell about?

_____

_____

Abbreviations for Days and Months

- Each day of the week can be written in a short way, called an **abbreviation**.

Mon. Tues. Wed. Thurs. Fri. Sat. Sun.

- Some months of the year can also be written in a short way. Notice that May, June, and July do not have a shortened form.

Jan.	**May**	**Sept.**
Feb.	**June**	**Oct.**
Mar.	**July**	**Nov.**
Apr.	**Aug.**	**Dec.**

The first Tues. in Mar.

Thinking Question
What does the short form of the word look like?

Write the abbreviation for each word.

1. Wednesday _____
2. December _____
3. Sunday _____
4. January _____
5. Monday _____
6. March _____
7. September _____
8. Tuesday _____
9. November _____

10. Saturday _____
11. February _____
12. July _____
13. June _____
14. October _____
15. Thursday _____
16. August _____
17. Friday _____
18. April _____

Schwa Vowel Sound

**Write each word. Draw a slash (/) to divide the word
between syllables. Then circle the quieter syllable
with the schwa sound.**

1. happen _____

2. about _____

3. talent _____

4. nickel _____

5. alone _____

6. dragonfly _____

**Now use the words you wrote above to complete the
sentences below.**

7. Luis has a lot of _____ for singing.

8. Sometimes Mia likes to be _____.

9. A _____ flew by.

10. What will _____ if it rains
    during the game?

11. Stan paid a _____ for a gumball.

12. Tell me _____ the picture you made.

Name _____ Date _____

Lesson 15
READER'S NOTEBOOK

Office Buckle
and Gloria
Independent Reading

Office Buckle and Gloria

Make a Poster

Use details and pictures from the book. Describe how Officer Buckle and Gloria learn to work together.

Read page 509. What did the children do while Officer Buckle gave talks without Gloria?

_____

Read pages 511–514. Now Officer Buckle has Gloria. How does Gloria help make his speeches better?

_____

_____

Read page 515. How did Officer Buckle change after Gloria joined him?

_____

Read page 523. What did Gloria do when Officer Buckle was not with her?

_____

_____

Abbreviations for Places

✎ **Write each underlined place correctly. Use abbreviations.**

1. I live on <u>Robin Road</u>.

_____

2. The pool is on <u>Shore drive</u>.

_____

3. Where is <u>Third avenue</u>?

_____

✎ **Write the name of the underlined words correctly. Write each abbreviation in its long form.**

4. Max lives on <u>North St</u>.

_____

5. Gloria visited a school on <u>Elm Ave.</u>

_____

6. <u>Rose Rd.</u> is only two blocks long.

_____

Name _____ Date _____

Lesson 15
READER'S NOTEBOOK

Officer Buckle
and Gloria
Vocabulary Strategies:
Root Words

Root Words

Underline the root word in each word. Use what you know about the root word to figure out the word's meaning. Complete each sentence by writing the word whose meaning fits the best.

> **Vocabulary**
>
> timer   unwrap   deepest   retake
> restacked   freezer   reddish   fielder

1. Joe didn't pass the math test. He will _____ the test next week.

2. I put the meat in the _____ because it must stay cold.

3. Sarah used a _____ to see how long she swam.

4. After he ran, his face was a _____ color.

5. You can't _____ your presents until your birthday.

6. Scientists want to learn what lives in the _____ part of the ocean.

7. Maria _____ the books on her desk.

8. Roger was a good _____, so he played in the outfield.

Abbreviations

Incorrect Abbreviations	Correct Abbreviations
dr levi	Dr. Levi
ms Jones	Ms. Jones
miss Oaks	Miss Oaks
River st	River St.
Tues	Tues.
jan.	Jan.

Proofread the paragraph. Fix any mistakes in abbreviations. Write the paragraph correctly on the lines.

My dad is a teacher. Kids call him mr Gary. On tues Dad read to his class. In mar they studied butterflies. Then on fri they visited a butterfly show. The show was on Main st.

_____

_____

_____

_____

_____

_____